1942

from
Kitty

Women's Wit
and Wisdom

Running Press
Philadelphia, Pennsylvania

Canadian representatives: General Publishing Co., Ltd.,
30 Lesmill Road, Don Mills, Ontario M3B 2T6.
International representatives: Worldwide Media Services, Inc.
115 East Twenty-third Street, New York, New York 10010

Library of Congress Catalog Card Number:
91–52696

ISBN 1-56138-037-7

This book may be ordered by mail from the publisher.
Please add $1.00 for postage and handling.
But try your bookstore first!
Running Press Book Publishers, 125 South Twenty-second
Street, Philadelphia, Pennsylvania 19103

IF YOU OBEY ALL THE RULES
YOU MISS ALL THE FUN.

KATHARINE HEPBURN, b. 1909
American actress

It's the good girls who keep the diaries; the bad girls never have the time.

Tallulah Bankhead (1903–1968)
American actress

In my sex fantasy, Nobody ever loves me for my mind.

NORA EPHRON, b. 1941
American writer

AN ARCHAEOLOGIST IS THE
BEST HUSBAND ANY WOMAN
CAN HAVE: THE OLDER SHE
GETS, THAT MORE INTERESTED
HE IS IN HER.

AGATHA CHRISTIE (1891–1976)
English writer

You don't know a woman until you have had a letter from her.

ADA LEVERSON (1862–1933)
English writer

I ALWAYS THOUGHT THAT IF I
WERE POPULAR I MUST BE
DOING SOMETHING WRONG.

SUZANNE VEGA, b. 1959
American singer and songwriter

To be meek, patient, tactful, modest, honorable, brave, is not to be either manly or womanly; it is to be humane.

JANE HARRISON (1850–1928)
English classical scholar

UNFORTUNATELY, SOMETIMES
PEOPLE DON'T HEAR YOU
UNTIL YOU SCREAM.

STEFANIE POWERS, b. 1943
American actress

A MAN HAS TO BE JOE
MCCARTHY TO BE CALLED
RUTHLESS. ALL A WOMAN HAS
TO DO IS PUT YOU ON HOLD.

MARLO THOMAS, b. 1943
American actress

THE IDEA OF STRICTLY
MINDING OUR OWN
BUSINESS IS MOLDY RUBBISH.
WHO COULD BE SO SELFISH?

MYRTIE BARKER, b. 1910
American columnist

THE TROUBLE WITH BEING IN
THE RAT RACE IS THAT EVEN IF
YOU WIN, YOU'RE STILL A RAT.

LILY TOMLIN, b. 1939
American actress and comedienne

WHEN A MAN GETS UP TO
SPEAK, PEOPLE LISTEN, THEN
LOOK. WHEN A WOMAN GETS
UP, PEOPLE *LOOK*; THEN, IF
THEY LIKE WHAT THEY SEE,
THEY LISTEN.

PAULINE FREDERICK (1908–1990)
American news correspondent

LET ME LISTEN TO ME AND
NOT TO THEM.

GERTRUDE STEIN (1874–1946)

American writer

I HAVE OFTEN WISHED I HAD
TIME TO CULTIVATE MODESTY.
. . . BUT I AM TOO BUSY
THINKING ABOUT MYSELF.

EDITH SITWELL (1887–1964)
English writer

If only one could tell true love from false love as one can tell mushrooms from toadstools.

Katherine Mansfield (1888–1923)
English writer

THE DARN TROUBLE WITH
CLEANING THE HOUSE IS IT
GETS DIRTY THE NEXT DAY
ANYWAY, SO SKIP A WEEK
IF YOU HAVE TO. THE
CHILDREN ARE THE MOST
IMPORTANT THING.

BARBARA BUSH, b. 1925
American First Lady

THE HARDEST TASK IN A GIRL'S
LIFE IS TO PROVE TO A MAN
THAT HIS INTENTIONS
ARE SERIOUS.

HELEN ROWLAND (1875–1950)
American writer

Anyone who's a great kisser I'm **always** interested in.

Cher, b. 1946
American actress and singer

My idea of a superwoman
is someone who scrubs
her own floors.

Bette Midler, b. 1945
American singer and actress

WHEN YOU HAVE A BABY,
YOU SET OFF AN EXPLOSION IN
YOUR MARRIAGE, AND WHEN
THE DUST SETTLES, YOUR
MARRIAGE IS DIFFERENT FROM
WHAT IT WAS. NOT BETTER,
NECESSARILY; NOT WORSE,
NECESSARILY; BUT DIFFERENT.

NORA EPHRON, b. 1941
American writer

Oh, life is a glorious
cycle of song, A medley
of extemporanea; And love
is a thing that can never
go wrong; And I am
Marie of Roumania.

Dorothy Parker (1893–1967)
American writer and humorist

THE AVERAGE MAN IS MORE
INTERESTED IN A WOMAN
WHO IS INTERESTED IN HIM
THAN HE IS IN A WOMAN WITH
BEAUTIFUL LEGS.

MARLENE DIETRICH, b. 1901
German-born American actress

If you want a baby, have a new one. Don't baby the old one.

Jessamyn West (1907–1984)
American writer

It goes without saying that you should never have more children than you have car windows.

Erma Bombeck, b. 1927
American writer and humorist

A WOMAN WITHOUT A MAN
IS LIKE A FISH WITHOUT
A BICYCLE.

GLORIA STEINEM, b. 1934
American feminist and writer

Oh, I'm so inadequate—
and I love myself!

MEG RYAN, b. 1962
American actress

We don't believe in
rheumatism and true
love until after the
first attack.

Marie von Ebner-Eschenbach
(1830–1916)
Austrian writer

WHENEVER YOU WANT TO
MARRY SOMEONE, GO HAVE
LUNCH WITH HIS EX-WIFE.

SHELLEY WINTERS, b. 1922
American actress

So many of us define ourselves by what we have, what we wear, what kind of house we live in and what kind of car we drive . . . . If you think of yourself as the woman in the Cartier watch and the Hermes scarf, a house fire will destroy not only your possessions but your self.

LINDA HENLEY, b. 1951
American writer

THE ONE IMPORTANT THING I HAVE LEARNED OVER THE YEARS IS THE DIFFERENCE BETWEEN TAKING ONE'S WORK SERIOUSLY AND TAKING ONE'S SELF SERIOUSLY. THE FIRST IS IMPERATIVE AND THE SECOND IS DISASTROUS.

MARGOT FONTEYN (1919–1991)
English dancer

It is the friends you can call up at 4 a.m. that matter.

Marlene Dietrich, b. 1901
German-born American actress

Personally, I think if a woman hasn't met the right man by the time she's 24, she may be lucky.

Deborah Kerr, b. 1921
Scottish-born American actress

Do not, on a rainy day, ask your child what he feels like doing, because I assure you that what he feels like doing, you won't feel like watching.

Fran Lebowitz, b. 1950
American writer

Never go to bed mad.
Stay up and fight.

Phyllis Diller, b. 1917
American comedienne and writer

Sometimes I wonder if men and women really suit each other. Perhaps they should live next door and just visit now and then.

Katharine Hepburn, b. 1909
American actress

ABSENCE DOES NOT MAKE
THE HEART GROW FONDER,
BUT IT SURE HEATS UP
THE BLOOD.

ELIZABETH ASHLEY, b. 1939
American actress

Love, like a chicken salad or restaurant hash, must be taken with blind faith or it loses its flavor.

HELEN ROWLAND (1875–1950)
American writer

Show me a woman who doesn't feel guilty and I'll show you a man.

Erica Jong, b. 1942
American writer and feminist

Whenever I dwell for any length of time on my own shortcomings, they gradually begin to seem mild, harmless, rather engaging little things, not at all like the staring defects in other people's characters.

Margaret Halsey, b. 1910
American writer

TIME WOUNDS ALL HEELS.

JANE ACE (1905–1974)
American radio personality

I DON'T SIT AROUND
THINKING THAT I'D LIKE TO
HAVE ANOTHER HUSBAND;
ONLY ANOTHER MAN WOULD
MAKE ME THINK THAT WAY.

LAUREN BACALL, b. 1924
American actress

WOMAN'S DISCONTENT INCREASES IN EXACT PROPORTION TO HER DEVELOPMENT.

ELIZABETH CADY STANTON
(1815–1902)
American suffragette

WHILE OTHERS MAY ARGUE
ABOUT WHETHER THE WORLD
ENDS WITH A BANG OR A
WHIMPER, I JUST WANT TO
MAKE SURE MINE DOESN'T
END WITH A WHINE.

BARBARA GORDON, b. 1935
American TV producer and writer

WHEN HE IS LATE FOR
DINNER AND I KNOW HE MUST
BE EITHER HAVING AN AFFAIR
OR LYING DEAD IN THE STREET,
I ALWAYS HOPE HE'S DEAD.

JUDITH VIORST, b. 1931
American writer

OF TWO EVILS CHOOSE THE PRETTIER.

CAROLYN WELLS (1870–1942)
American writer

It's never too late—in fiction or in life—to revise.

NANCY THAYER, b. 1943
American writer

I THINK THE ONE LESSON I
HAVE LEARNED IS THAT
THERE IS NO SUBSTITUTE
FOR PAYING ATTENTION.

DIANE SAWYER, b. 1945
American journalist

I'D LIKE TO GROW VERY OLD
AS SLOWLY AS POSSIBLE.

IRENE MAYER SELZNICK (1907–1990)
Stage producer

AGE DOES NOT PROTECT YOU FROM LOVE. BUT LOVE, TO SOME EXTENT, PROTECTS YOU FROM AGE.

JEANNE MOREAU, b. 1929
French actress

THE THING WOMEN HAVE GOT
TO LEARN IS THAT NOBODY
GIVES YOU POWER. YOU JUST
TAKE IT.

ROSEANNE BARR, b. 1952
American comedienne and actress

MAN FORGIVES WOMAN ANYTHING SAVE THE WIT TO OUTWIT HIM.

MINNA ANTRIM
19th-century Irish writer

I LIKE A VIEW BUT I LIKE TO SIT
WITH MY BACK TURNED TO IT.

GERTRUDE STEIN (1874–1946)

American writer

Kids learn more from example than anything you say. I'm convinced they learn very early not to hear anything you say, but watch what you do.

Jane Pauley, b. 1950
American journalist

I'm not denyin' the women are foolish: God Almighty made 'em to match the men.

George Eliot
(Mary Ann Evans, 1819–1880)
English writer

TRUE STRENGTH IS DELICATE.

LOUISE NEVELSON (1899–1988)

American sculptor

WERE WOMEN MEANT TO DO EVERYTHING—WORK AND HAVE BABIES?

CANDICE BERGEN, b. 1946
American actress

A MAN'S HOME MAY SEEM
TO BE HIS CASTLE ON THE
OUTSIDE; INSIDE IT IS MORE
OFTEN HIS NURSERY.

CLARE BOOTH LUCE (1903–1987)
American diplomat and writer

If I'm too strong for some people, that's their problem.

Glenda Jackson, b. 1936
English actress

It is better to die on
your feet than to live
on your knees.

Dolores Ibárruri (1895–1989)
Spanish communist leader

It is sad to grow old but nice to ripen

BRIGITTE BARDOT, b. 1934
French actress

LUCK IS A MATTER OF
PREPARATION MEETING
OPPORTUNITY.

OPRAH WINFREY, b. 1953
American talk show host and actress

THE ONLY INTERESTING
ANSWERS ARE THOSE WHICH
DESTROY THE QUESTIONS.

SUSAN SONTAG, b. 1933
American writer and social critic

MEN ARE TAUGHT TO
APOLOGIZE FOR THEIR
WEAKNESSES, WOMEN FOR
THEIR STRENGTHS.

LOIS WYSE, b. 1926
American advertising executive

You grow up the day you have your first real laugh at yourself.

ETHEL BARRYMORE (1879–1959)
American actress

THE PHRASE "WORKING MOTHER" IS REDUNDANT.

JANE SELLMAN
20th-century American writer

WHEN YOU'RE IN LOVE, YOU PUT UP WITH THINGS THAT, WHEN YOU'RE OUT OF LOVE, YOU CITE.

MISS MANNERS (JUDITH MARTIN),
b. 1938
American writer

THE WAY I SEE IT, IF YOU
WANT THE RAINBOW, YOU
GOTTA PUT UP WITH THE RAIN.

DOLLY PARTON, b. 1946
American singer and actress

Marrying a man is like buying something you've been admiring for a long time in a shop window. You may love it when you get it home, but it doesn't always go with everything else.

Jean Kerr, b. 1923
American playwright

A WOMAN MAY DEVELOP
WRINKLES AND CELLULITE,
LOSE HER WAISTLINE, HER
BUSTLINE, HER ABILITY TO
BEAR A CHILD, EVEN HER SENSE
OF HUMOR, BUT NONE OF
THAT IMPLIES A LOSS OF
SEXUALITY, HER FEMININITY. . . .

BARBARA GORDON, b. 1935
American TV producer and writer

I'M SUGGESTING WE CALL SEX
SOMETHING ELSE, AND IT
SHOULD INCLUDE EVERYTHING
FROM KISSING TO SITTING
CLOSE TOGETHER.

SHERE HITE, b. 1942
American writer

THE WAY TO KEEP CHILDREN
AT HOME IS TO MAKE HOME
A PLEASANT ATMOSPHERE—
AND TO LET THE AIR OUT
OF THE TIRES.

DOROTHY PARKER (1893–1967)
American writer

I DON'T BELIEVE MAN IS
WOMAN'S NATURAL ENEMY.
PERHAPS HIS LAWYER IS.

SHANA ALEXANDER, b. 1925
American writer

FROM BIRTH TO AGE 18 A GIRL NEEDS GOOD PARENTS. FROM 18 TO 35 SHE NEEDS GOOD LOOKS. FROM 35 TO 55 SHE NEEDS A GOOD PERSONALITY. FROM 55 ON, SHE NEEDS GOOD CASH.

SOPHIE TUCKER (1884–1966)
American singer

GROAN AND FORGET IT.

JESSAMYN WEST (1907–1984)
American writer

THE MOTHER IS THE MOST
PRECIOUS POSSESSION OF THE
NATION, SO PRECIOUS THAT
SOCIETY ADVANCES ITS
HIGHEST WELL-BEING WHEN
IT PROTECTS THE FUNCTIONS
OF THE MOTHER.

ELLEN KEY (1849–1926)
Swedish writer

My TRUE FRIENDS HAVE
ALWAYS GIVEN ME THAT
SUPREME PROOF OF DEVOTION,
A SPONTANEOUS AVERSION
FOR THE MAN I LOVED.

COLETTE (1873–1954)
French writer

Ideally, couples need three lives; one for him, one for her, and one for them together.

Jacqueline Bisset, b. 1946
English actress

I LIVE BY A MAN'S CODE,
DESIGNED TO FIT A MAN'S
WORLD, YET AT THE SAME
TIME I NEVER FORGET THAT
A WOMAN'S FIRST JOB IS TO
CHOOSE THE RIGHT SHADE
OF LIPSTICK.

CAROLE LOMBARD (1908–1942)
American actress

How many cares one loses when one decides not to be something, but to be someone.

Coco Chanel (1883–1971)
French couturière

. . . A MAN SHOULD KISS HIS
WIFE'S NAVEL EVERY DAY.

NELL KIMBALL (1854–1934)
American madam and writer

[BEING A PARENT] IS
TOUGH. IF YOU JUST WANT A
WONDERFUL LITTLE CREATURE
TO LOVE, YOU CAN GET
A PUPPY.

BARBARA WALTERS, b. 1931
American journalist

THE ULTIMATE LESSON ALL
OF US HAVE TO LEARN IS
UNCONDITIONAL LOVE,
WHICH INCLUDES NOT
ONLY OTHERS BUT OUR-
SELVES AS WELL.

ELISABETH KUBLER-ROSS, b. 1926
Swiss-born psychiatrist and writer

I WAS NOT A CLASSIC MOTHER.
BUT MY KIDS WERE NEVER
PALMED OFF TO BOARDING
SCHOOL. SO, I DIDN'T BAKE
COOKIES. YOU CAN BUY
COOKIES, BUT YOU
CAN'T BUY LOVE.

RAQUEL WELCH, b. 1940
American actress

IT IS POSSIBLE THAT BLONDES
ALSO PREFER GENTLEMEN.

MAMIE VAN DOREN, b. 1933
American singer

LOVE IS A FIRE. BUT WHETHER IT IS GOING TO WARM YOUR HEARTH OR BURN DOWN YOUR HOUSE, YOU CAN NEVER TELL.

JOAN CRAWFORD (1906–1977)
American actress

Self-pity in its early stages
is as snug as a feather
mattress. Only when
it hardens does it
become uncomfortable.

Maya Angelou, b. 1928
American writer and entertainer

A CHILD OF ONE CAN BE
TAUGHT NOT TO DO CERTAIN
THINGS SUCH AS TOUCH A
HOT STOVE, TURN ON THE
GAS, PULL LAMPS OFF THEIR
TABLES BY THEIR CORDS, OR
WAKE MOMMY BEFORE NOON.

JOAN RIVERS, b. 1933
American entertainer

IF LOVE IS THE ANSWER,
COULD YOU PLEASE
REPHRASE THE QUESTION?

LILY TOMLIN, b. 1939
American actress and comedienne

Love: Quotations from the Heart

Love Sonnets of Shakespeare

Motherhood

The Night Before Christmas

Quotable Women

Sherlock Holmes:
Two Complete Adventures

Tales from the Arabian Nights

Tales of Peter Rabbit

The Velveteen Rabbit

The Wit and Wisdom of Mark Twain

Women's Wit and Wisdom

This book has been bound using
handcraft methods, and Smythe-
sewn to ensure durability.

The dust jacket was designed and
illustrated by Toby Schmidt.
The interior was designed
by Skagg.
The interior illustrations are
by Liz Vodges.
The text was typeset in Gill Sans
by Commcor Communications
Corporation, Philadelphia,
Pennsylvania.